# Languages of the World
# German

## Sarah Medina

Heinemann Library
Chicago, Illinois

**www.heinemannraintree.com**
Visit our website to find out more information about Heinemann-Raintree books.

**To order:**
☎ Phone 888-454-2279
🖳 Visit www.heinemannraintree.com to browse our catalog and order online.

Edited by Dan Nunn, Rebecca Rissman, and
   Catherine Veitch
Designed by Marcus Bell
Picture research by Ruth Blair
Production by Victoria Fitzgerald
Originated by Capstone Global Library Ltd
Printed and bound in China by South China Printing
   Company Ltd

15 14 13 12 11
10 9 8 7 6 5 4 3 2 1

**Library of Congress Cataloging-in-Publication Data**
Medina, Sarah, 1960-
   German / Sarah Medina.
      p. cm.—(Languages of the world)
   Includes bibliographical references and index.
   ISBN 978-1-4329-5184-9 (hc)—ISBN 978-1-4329-5186-3 (pb) 1. German language—Textbooks for foreign speakers—English. 2. German language—Grammar. 3. German language—Spoken German. I. Title.
   PF3129.E5M43 2012
   438.2'421—dc21                2010043792

**Acknowledgments**
We would like to thank the following for permission to reproduce photographs: Alamy pp. 12 (© Nordicphotos), 23 (© Golden Pixels LLC); Corbis pp. 17 (© Juice Images), 19 (© Adam Woolfitt), 26 (© Envision); iStockphoto p. 8 (© Tamara Murray); Photolibrary pp. 11 (imagebroker. net), 27 (Japan Travel Bureau), 29 (imagebroker.net); Shutterstock pp. 5 (© Losevsky Pavel), 6 (© Ronald Sumners), 7 (© Tatiana Belova), 9 (© Monkey Business Images), 10 (© blueking), 13 (© SergiyN), 14 (© Monkey Business Images), 15 (© Rob Marmion), 16 (© Tatjana Strelkova), 18 (© Stephen Finn), 20 (© get4net), 21 (© wavebreakmedia ltd), 22 (© oliveromg), 24 (© Monkey Business Images), 25 (© Jiri Pavlik), 28 (© Anatoliy Samara).

Cover photograph of a laughing boy reproduced with permission of Photolibrary (Stockbrokerxtra Images).

We would like to thank Regina Irwin for her invaluable help in the preparation of this book.

Every effort has been made to contact copyright holders of material reproduced in this book. Any omissions will be rectified in subsequent printings if notice is given to the publisher.

All the Internet addresses (URLs) given in this book were valid at the time of going to press. However, due to the dynamic nature of the Internet, some addresses may have changed, or sites may have changed or ceased to exist since publication. While the author and publisher regret any inconvenience this may cause readers, no responsibility for any such changes can be accepted by either the author or the publisher.

# Contents

German words are in italics, *like this.* You can find out how to say them by looking in the pronunciation guide.

# German Around the World

German is the language that most people speak in Germany, Austria, and Switzerland. Most people speak German in Liechtenstein and Luxemburg, too.

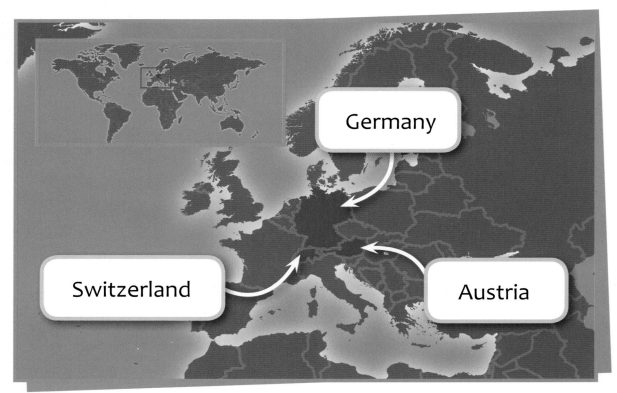

More than 90,000 books are written in German every year.

There are also people who speak German all around the world. They can be found from Italy in Europe to the United States in North America, and Argentina in South America.

# Who Speaks German?

German is the main language of about 120 million people around the world. "German" in German is *Deutsch*.

In Switzerland people call German *Switzerdütsch*.

Students in many countries learn German at school.

German can sound different from one country to the next. People sometimes use different words for the same thing, too. The word for "tomatoes" is *Tomaten* in Germany and *Paradeiser* in Austria.

# German and English

Some words, such as *Hamster*, are the same in German and in English. Other words are very alike. Can you guess the meanings of the words below?

*Mutter    Mann    Kalender    Papier*
(See page 32 for answers.)

The German word *Glockenspiel* is also used in English for the same instrument.

A hamburger in English is a *Hamburger* in German, too!

Words that name things are called nouns. In German, nouns always start with a capital letter. For example, "dog" in English is *Hund* in German.

# Learning German

German uses the same alphabet as English, but it has 30 letters instead of 26. The extra letters are circled in red below.

a ä b c d e
f g h i j k l
m n o ö p
q r s ß t u
ü v w x y z

"Cheese" in German is *Käse*. The two dots over the "a" make it sound like "kay-se" instead of "kah-se."

The letter ß is sometimes used instead of writing "ss." The dots above ä, ö, and ü are called an *Umlaut*. An *Umlaut* changes the sound of a letter.

# Saying Hello and Goodbye

People who do not know each other usually shake hands when they say hello. In Switzerland, family and friends may give each other three kisses on the cheeks.

**How to say it**
handshake = *Händedruck*
kiss = *Kuss*

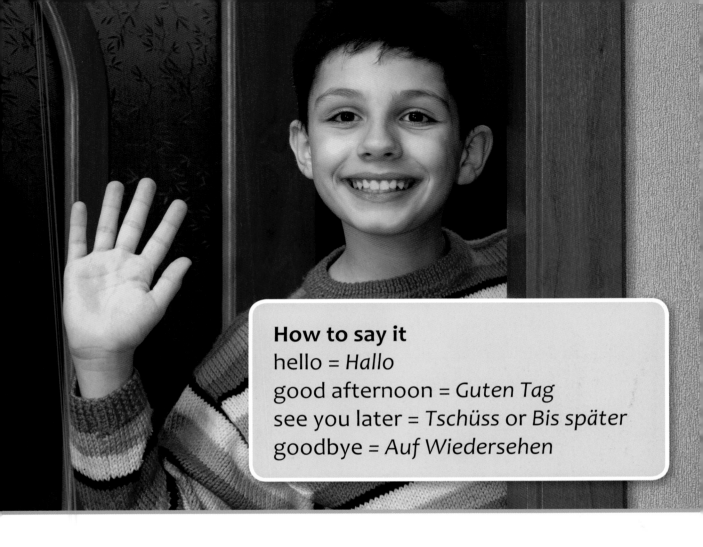

**How to say it**
hello = *Hallo*
good afternoon = *Guten Tag*
see you later = *Tschüss* or *Bis später*
goodbye = *Auf Wiedersehen*

When people meet, they may say "*Hallo*" or "*Guten Tag*." "*Auf Wiedersehen*" means "goodbye", but family and friends often say "*Tschüss*" or "*Bis später*", too.

# Talking About Yourself

When people meet others for the first time, they usually give their name. They may say "*Ich heiße Sarah*" or "*Mein Name ist Sarah.*"

**How to say it**
I'm called … = *Ich heiße …*
My name is … = *Mein Name ist …*

**How to say it**
I'm from ... = *Ich komme aus ...*
I live in ... = *Ich wohne in ...*

People often say where they come from.
For example, *"Ich komme aus Deutschland."*
("I come from Germany.") They may say
where they live. For example, *"Ich wohne in
London."* ("I live in London.")

# Asking About Others

To ask someone what their name is, you say "*Wie heißt Du?*" or "*Wie ist Dein Name?*" If you are talking to someone older, use "*Wie heißen Sie?*" to be polite.

**How to say it**
What's your name? = *Wie heißt Du?* or
*Wie ist Dein Name?*

**How to say it**
Where are you from?
= *Woher kommst Du?*
Where do you live?
= *Wo wohnst Du?*

To ask someone where they come from people usually say "*Woher kommst Du?*" If they want to know where someone lives they say "*Wo wohnst Du?*"

# At Home

In Germany most people live in apartments instead of houses. In cities some people share an outside space on some land near their apartment block.

**How to say it**
apartment = *Wohnung*
house = *Haus*
garden = *Garten*

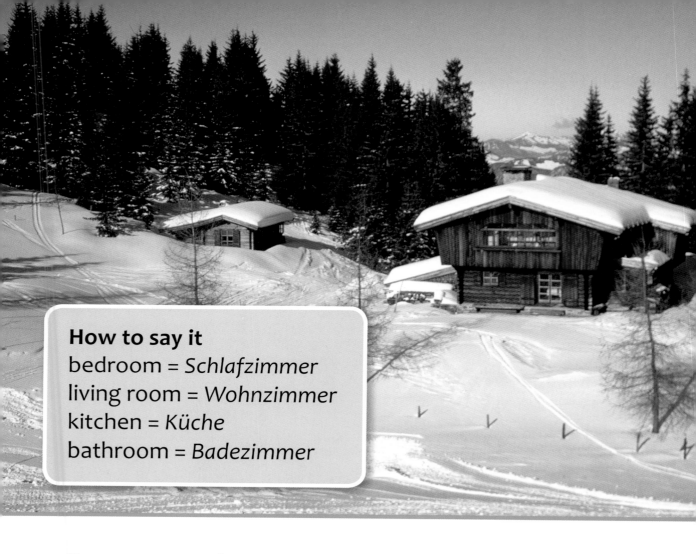

**How to say it**
bedroom = *Schlafzimmer*
living room = *Wohnzimmer*
kitchen = *Küche*
bathroom = *Badezimmer*

Some people in Austria live in chalets. Chalets have all the rooms that normal houses have, but they are built mainly from wood.

# Family Life

In German-speaking countries families are usually quite small. Parents may have one or two children. Some children live with just one parent.

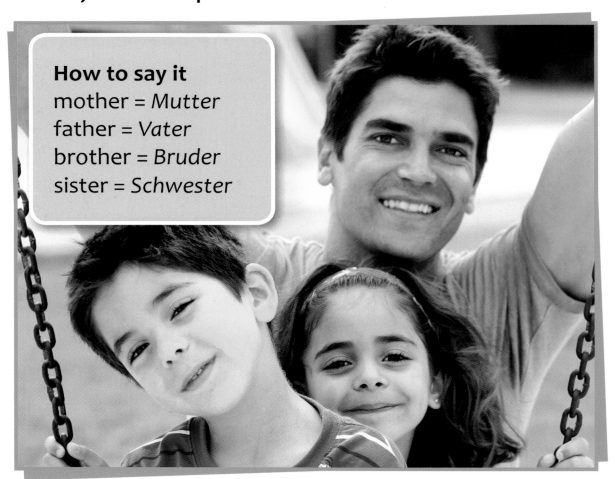

**How to say it**
mother = *Mutter*
father = *Vater*
brother = *Bruder*
sister = *Schwester*

Grandparents are important members of the family. They are usually part of celebrations like Christmas and birthdays. Some grandparents live with the whole family all the time.

# At School

Most German pupils only go to school in the morning. They go home for lunch. They usually have lots of homework to do in the afternoon.

**How to say it**
school = *Schule*
homework = *Hausaufgaben*

**How to say it**
music = *Musik*
instrument = *Instrument*
violin = *Geige*

In the small country of Liechtenstein, there is a special music school for children. Pupils can learn to play instruments like the violin. They perform in many concerts.

# Sports

In Germany, people love sports. There are thousands of sports clubs across the country. Soccer is the most popular sport for many adults and children.

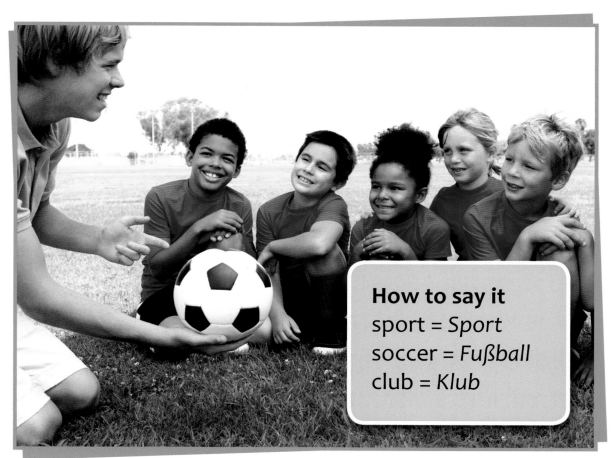

**How to say it**
sport = *Sport*
soccer = *Fußball*
club = *Klub*

Many people in Switzerland enjoy skiing or snowboarding. They are lucky because there are snow-covered mountains all around that they can go to for the weekend or during vacations.

# Food

In Germany, lunch is the main meal of the day. People often have three courses. The evening meal is much lighter—perhaps some soup with bread, cheese, sausage, and ham.

**How to say it**
soup = *Suppe*
bread = *Brot*
cheese = *Käse*
sausage = *Wurst*
ham = *Schinken*

**How to say it**
café = *Café*
coffee = *Kaffee*
cake = *Kuchen*
pastries = *Gebäck*

In Austria there are many cafés. People go there to drink coffee, to eat cakes and pastries, to relax with friends, or to read. They even go there to work.

# Clothes

Many people in German-speaking countries relax in clothes like T-shirts and jeans. People usually wear dressier clothes for work, like suits and shirts.

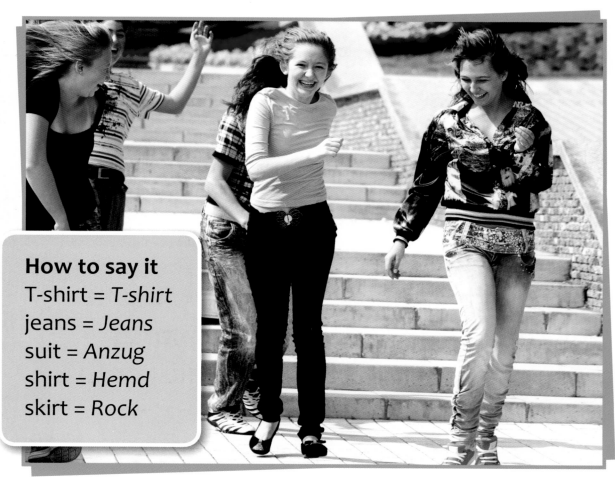

**How to say it**
T-shirt = *T-shirt*
jeans = *Jeans*
suit = *Anzug*
shirt = *Hemd*
skirt = *Rock*

In the German mountains, called the Alps, boys used to wear short leather trousers called *Lederhosen*. Nowadays, *Lederhosen* are only worn at special festivals like the *Oktoberfest*.

29

# Pronunciation Guide

| English | German | Pronunciation |
|---------|--------|---------------|
| apartment | Wohnung | Voh-nung |
| Austria | Österreich | Urs-ter-raic |
| bathroom | Badezimmer | Bar-deh-tsim-ah |
| bedroom | Schlafzimmer | Shlarf-tsim-ah |
| bread | Brot | Broh-at |
| brother | Bruder | Broo-dah |
| café | Café | Kaf-ay |
| cake | Kuchen | Koo-khen |
| cheese | Käse | Kaiy-sah |
| club | Klub | Kloob |
| coffee | Kaffee | Kaf-ay |
| family | Familie | Fam-eel-ee-ya |
| father | Vater | Fah-tah |
| festival | Fest | Fest |
| garden | Garten | Gard-uhn |
| Germany | Deutschland | Doych-land |
| good afternoon | Guten Tag | Goo-ten tagg |
| grandfather | Großvater | Groas-fah-tah |
| grandmother | Großmutter | Groas-moo-tah |
| ham | Schinken | Shin-kan |
| handshake | Händedruck | Hen-dee-drook |
| hello | Hallo | Hal-oh |
| homework | Hausaufgaben | Hows-owf-gah-ban |
| house | Haus | Hows |
| I live in ... | Ich wohne in ... | Ik vo-nah in |
| I'm called ... | Ich heiße ... | Ik high-sah |

| | | |
|---|---|---|
| I'm from … | Ich komme aus … | Ik kom-ah ows |
| instrument | Instrument | In-stroo-ment |
| jeans | Jeans | Jeens |
| kiss | Kuss | Koo-s |
| kitchen | Küche | Koo-kah |
| leather | Leder | Laiy-dah |
| living room | Wohnzimmer | Vo-an-tsim-ah |
| mother | Mutter | Moo-tah |
| music | Musik | Moo-zeek |
| My name is … | Mein Name ist … | My-n nah-me ist |
| pastries | Gebäck | Guh-bek |
| sausage | Wurst | Voor-st |
| school | Schule | Shoo-lah |
| see you later | Tschüss | Choos |
| see you later | Bis später | Bis shpay-tah |
| shirt | Hemd | Hemmed |
| sister | Schwester | Shwess-tah |
| skiing | Skilaufen | Shee-low-fen |
| skirt | Rock | Rock |
| snowboarding | Snowboarden | Sno-bor-dan |
| soccer | Fußball | Foos-bal |
| soup | Suppe | Zoo-pah |
| sport | Sport | Shport |
| suit | Anzug | An-tsoo-g |
| T-shirt | T-shirt | Tee-shoort |
| trousers | Hosen | Hoa-zen |
| violin | Geige | Guy-gah |
| What's your name? | Wie heißt Du? | Vee high-st doo |
| What's your name? | Wie ist Dein Name? | Vee ist dine nah-me |
| Where are you from? | Woher kommst Du? | Vo-hair kom-st doo |
| Where do you live? | Wo wohnst Du? | Vo voh-nst doo |

# Find Out More

## Book

Alcraft, Rob. *A Visit to Germany*. Chicago:
Heineman Library, 2008.

## Websites

kids.nationalgeographic.com/kids/places/find/germany/

www.ukgermanconnection.org/kids/?location_id=868

## Index

---

**Meanings of the words on page 8**

*Mutter* = mother     *Mann* = man

*Kalender* = calendar     *Papier* = paper

---